THE SIXTH FORM COLLEGE, SOLIHULL
THE LEARNING CENTRE

D0364640

SOLIHULL
A Pictorial History

St Alphege's church

SOLIHULL

A Pictorial History

Sue Bates

CHECKED   JUL 2008

Phillimore

Rec	21 11 05
Stock no.	54543
Class	
	942.48
Labels	
T	

1991

Published by
PHILLIMORE & CO. LTD.
Shopwyke Hall, Chichester, Sussex

© Sue Bates 1991

ISBN 0 85033 784 4

Printed and bound in Great Britain by
BIDDLES LTD.
Guildford, Surrey

For my parents, Ted and Dora Hicken

List of Illustrations

Frontispiece: St Alphege's church

THE TOWN

1. Extract from O.S. map, 1888
2. Solihull High Street, *c.*1829
3. Solihull High Street, *c.*1900
4. Old *George and Dragon*, before 1887
5. High Street
6. High Street, *c.*1915
7. Top of High Street, *c.*1913
8. High Street, from Church tower, 1910
9. High Street
10. Post Office
11. Manor House
12. The Gables
13. Houses in High Street, *c.*1870
14. Houses in High Street, *c.*1870
15. High Street, 1897
16. High Street, *c.*1912
17. The Square, *c.*1820
18. The Square, *c.*1870
19. The 'End Houses', before 1921
20. St Alphege's school, Park Road, *c.*1905
21. Park Road in the 1880s
22. Malvern House
23. New Road, *c.*1926
24. Solihull School, *c.*1905
25. Solihull School, after 1917
26. Warwick Road, after 1882
27. Warwick Road
28. Drury Lane
29. Mill Lane, *c.*1911
30. Cottages in Drury Lane, *c.*1900
31. Cottages in Mill Lane, *c.*1948
32. Warwick Road Post Office, *c.*1918
33. Union Workhouse
34. Poplar Road
35. Lloyds Bank and the old Council House
36. Station Road, *c.*1912
37. Solihull station, *c.*1864
38. Solihull station, before 1932
39. Solihull station with passengers

THE COUNTRY

40. Extract from O.S. map, 1888
41. Ravenshaw
42. Sandals Bridge
43. Streetsbrook Road, *c.*1907
44. Blossomfield Road, *c.*1910
45. Church Hill, *c.*1915
46. Rectory meadow, 1897
47. Malvern Park Farm, *c.*1900
48. Evans Convalescent Home, 1911
49. Silhill Hall
50. Silhill Hall: interior
51. Homer Road, *c.*1900
52. Ashleigh Road, *c.*1910
53. Lode Lane, *c.*1900
54. Canal bridge, Lode Lane, *c.*1905
55. The *Anchor Inn* and Grand Union Canal
56. Gas Board workers at the *Anchor Inn*
57. Olton Watermill, Lode Lane, 1913
58. Henwood Mill
59. Henwood Mill
60. Moat Farm, Lode Lane
61. Berry Hall Farm, *c.*1900
62. New Berry Hall
63. Ravenshaw Hall, *c.*1947
64. Timber yard, Lode Lane

VILLAGE CHARACTERS

65. James Holliday
66. Granny Leeson
67. Barber Hopkins
68. Thomas Horne
69. Hugh Taylor Trinder, *c.*1930
70. Arthur Hobbins
71. Hobbins' advertisement, *c.*1911
72. Wedding of Miss Winnie Warner, 1920
73. Residents of Ramsgate Cottages
74. Solihull Cricket Team
75. Solihull Football Club

SOME HOUSES AND FAMILIES

76. Malvern Hall: front view
77. Malvern Hall: rear view
78. Hillfield Hall
79. The Hawes family, *c.*1610
80. Solihull Rectory, before 1833
81. The Revd. Charles Curtis
82. Solihull Rectory, *c.*1900
83. The Revd. Archer Clive, 1847
84. Caroline Clive, *c.*1860
85. The Old Priory before 1889
86. The Priory, post 1889
87. Mathews family
88. Silhill House, *c.*1853
89. Silhill House garden
90. Tudor Grange
91. Sir Alfred Bird

Acknowledgements

I would like to record grateful thanks to all those who have helped me to prepare and research this work, including the following: John Marks, Dora Mason, Dr. Denis Gray and Solihull Society of Arts for loan of their photographs, and Dr. Bob McKee, Director of Libraries and Arts for Solihull Metropolitan Borough, for allowing me access to the material in the Local Studies Collection in Solihull Library. I am especially grateful to Mr. Charles Lines for allowing me access to his photographs and unpublished records, and to Joy Woodall for her help and support. Special thanks are also due to my father, Ted Hicken, for the original photography in the book and for copying many of the older photographs. Other photographic work has been done by June Lawrence and my husband, John Bates, who has given me much support, listening patiently to my agonising over the choice of photographs and helping me to struggle with the word processor. I should point out that all opinions, conclusions and mistakes are mine alone!

Finally I would like to pay tribute to the early pioneer photographers of Solihull – in particular Edwin and Hugh Trinder, Arthur Hobbins, David Jewsbury and Cliff Joiner – without whose work this book would not have been possible.

Illustration Acknowledgements

Author, 2, 11, 16, 24, 26, 41, 43, 48, 52, 53, 57, 61, 82, 95-7, 101, 116, 117, 134, 137, 139, 141-5, 150, 151, 165, 169, 170-2; Graham Roberts, 153, 159; Mrs. Simmons, 154; Mrs. Lippiatt, 128; Birmingham Library Services Local Studies Department, 126, 127; Mrs. Pinfold, 56, 160; John Marks, 7, 9, 22, 25, 27, 28, 30, 32, 113, 135; Knowle Society, 155, 156; Mrs. Dora Mason, 60, 72, 147, 149; Featherstones' Antiquarian Magazine, 112; Ordnance Survey, 1, 40; Christ Church, Solihull, 118-20; Tim Booth, 59; Hannett, 76; Miss Griffiths, 77; Lady Mary Clive, 83, 84; 'Joiner Collection', Solihull Library, Frontispiece, 3, 8, 15, 19, 20, 44, 46, 47, 50, 62, 71, 74, 85, 89, 92, 93, 98, 102, 104, 106, 108, 109, 121, 161-4, 168; Solihull Library, 6, 10, 17, 18, 23, 34-6, 38, 45, 51, 54, 55, 64, 67, 69, 70, 73, 75, 78, 79, 86, 90, 91, 94, 99, 103, 107, 114, 115, 123-5, 130, 131, 136, 138, 140, 157, 158, 167; Warwick County Record Office, 39, 65, 80, 81; Charles Line, 4, 5, 12-14, 21, 99; Solihull Metropolitan Borough, 164; Solihull Society of Arts, 31, 37, 42, 49, 58, 63, 66, 88, 103, 110, 129, 146, 148; Mrs. Linda Allen, 152; Dr Denis Gray, 29, 33, 122, 132, 133; St Margaret's church, 87.

Introduction

Through the centuries the name 'Solihull' has been applied to several different geographical areas including medieval borough, parish, town, and through various stages of local government administration to the present Metropolitan Borough. Most of these areas have had different boundaries. This book will concentrate on the town of Solihull, but it is necessary also to consider its position in the context of the wider area now bearing the same name.

The name 'Solihull' was first recorded *c*.1170-80 in the Red Book of the Exchequer, and means muddy, or miry, hill. The name derives from the Anglo-Saxon and has had several variant spellings. Perhaps it would be useful to state at the outset that the traditional pronunciation is *Sol* as in 'sole' not as in 'solitude'. A once popular variation, recorded in West's *Directory of Warwickshire* (1830) as the 'general pronunciation' was Silhill (hence Silhillian), but this version is little used today. The hill is the present Church Hill, once much steeper than the modern road and extremely muddy in wet weather due to its composition of stiff, red clay. The town was founded in the late 12th century by the lords of the manor of Ulverlei, in which the new town was situated. Before that time the centre of the manor was about two miles away at Olton.

Ulverlei was an Anglo-Saxon manor, situated in the Forest of Arden, a vast area of ancient woodland which once covered much of the north-western part of the county of Warwickshire. Although the popular image of Arden is of a dense forest, the reality was a mixture of natural clearings and woodland. In fact, some medieval 'forests' had no trees at all, but the meaning of the word has changed over the centuries which has led to confusion in the modern period. A forest was originally an area where deer were protected under forest law. Much of the Arden woodland survived as a natural feature until the 18th century, when quantities of timber were cut to supply the needs of the ironmasters.

Arden was never a legal forest under forest laws, but it was a recognisable region of woodland which formed a natural defence against the invasions of the conquering tribes of Angles and Saxons. It was not until the seventh century that the original British settlers of the Arden plateau retreated to Wales after the defeat of their allies by Saxon forces, who had advanced along the Severn Valley to fight the battle of Bangor Iscoed and thus cut the line of communication with Wales. This left the way clear for settlement of the plateau by the Angles (or English) who had advanced along the Tame Valley, which afforded a ready means of access for the invaders who eventually held most of the plateau while the Saxons infiltrated from the south-west. It is interesting to note that the ancient boundary between the dioceses of Lichfield and Worcester (in existence by 629 and unchanged until 1836) marked the frontier between the lands of the Angles and those of the Saxons respectively.

At the time of the Norman Conquest in 1066 the manor of Ulverlei was held by Edwin, Earl of Mercia. Edwin was King Harold's brother-in-law and supported Harold against both the campaigns by the Norwegians and the Normans. Together with his brother

Morcar, Edwin led an army north early in 1066 to fight against the invading Norwegians near York. Edwin was defeated, but had weakened the enemy, so that Harold was able to win the Battle of Stamford Bridge. Harold was forced to march south almost immediately to fight against the Normans, but Edwin and Morcar failed to raise another army in time to reach Hastings. The brothers eventually submitted to William I, realising the collapse of the Saxon cause. However, in 1071 Edwin joined forces with anti-Norman rebels in the north of England, and was caught and killed. Morcar joined Hereward the Wake on the Isle of Ely, and although he too was eventually captured he was imprisoned not executed. The manor of Ulverlei, together with all the other estates belonging to both brothers, therefore reverted to the King.

By the time of the Domesday Survey, ordered by King William in 1086, the manor was held 'of the king' by the princess Christina, a member of the Saxon royal family. Christina's grandfather was Edmund Ironside, son of Ethelred the 'Unready', who was succeeded as 'King of all England' by Cnut, and her brother was Edgar Atheling. After Harold's defeat and death at the Battle of Hastings, Edgar made a brief and unsuccessful attempt to overthrow William, but soon submitted to the king in 1067, and fled to Scotland with his mother and sisters, to the protection of King Malcolm. In 1070 Margaret, Christina's sister, married Malcolm and became Queen of Scotland. Like her great-uncle, Edward the Confessor, Margaret had a saintly disposition, and she was later to be canonised, becoming St Margaret of Scotland. In 1073 Malcolm made an agreement with William I in which he became William's vassal. It is possible that this agreement also made provision for Christina, who was unmarried. Apart from Ulverlei, Christina also held the manors of Arlei and Icentone (Long Itchington) at the time of the Domesday Survey. These manors were all held from the king, and this led the 18th-century Birmingham historian, William Hutton, to suppose that Christina was William's mistress. It seems more likely, however, that William was merely fulfilling his obligations to his vassal by providing for Malcolm's family. It is unlikely that Christina actually lived at Ulverlei, and later in 1087 she retired to a convent, and eventually became Abbess of Romsey Abbey.

The manor of Ulverlei was then given to Ralph de Limesi, a Norman knight who was probably William's nephew. From this family the manor passed by marriage to the de Oddingsell family, through Basilia (daughter of John de Limesi) who married Hugh de Oddingsell in 1213. Hugh was a soldier, and held the barony of Ulverlei by 'knight service'. Hugh died in 1238 and his younger son William inherited Ulverlei. It was William de Oddingsell who was granted a charter by King Henry III in 1242 which allowed a weekly market and an annual three day fair from 18-20 April (to coincide with the feast day of St Alphege, to whom Solihull parish church is dedicated) and to be held in the recently established settlement of Solihull.

The location of Solihull was carefully chosen, and was specially created on the eastern side of the manor, near the boundary with the neighbouring manor of Longdon. This site was advantageous as it was at the intersection of two important ancient roads. One road linked Birmingham and Warwick and the other, more important, route came from Worcester through Droitwich to Coventry, and beyond. Both routes were much frequented by traders, and Coventry was the most important trade centre in the medieval West Midlands. Droitwich had long been a major salt-producing centre, and this road was probably one of the ancient saltways of England. It is now generally accepted that Solihull was a 'planted borough', created for the purpose of trade. There is evidence to suggest that the town was well planned, with burgage plots laid out before the town was ready for occupation. Burgage tenure meant that tenants were freemen, paying rent for their properties, unlike villeins who held their land in return for labour service and were not freemen. Streets were laid out in a grid pattern, which may still be detected today in the High Street, Poplar Road, Mill Lane, Drury Lane and Warwick Road.

In the early years Solihull flourished, and in 1285 William de Oddingsell II obtained a confirmation of the charter of Henry III. The market charter was renewed again in 1320 by the Bishop of Ely, who was by this time lord of the manor. Initially, in the 13th and 14th centuries, the borough seems to have continued to prosper. There is evidence to suggest tradesmen and craftsmen such as cloth-makers, leather and metal-workers, bakers, sawyers, and brewers. In the long term, however, the town did not continue to expand. Some general market trading continued, but the town did not flourish in the same way as its close neighbour Birmingham, and by the end of the 14th century had begun a steady decline in importance. This may have been a result of the fact that after the de Oddingsell family died out the manor had no resident lord to encourage expansion. However, Solihull was not alone in this decline of its business and influence: Penelope Corfield in *The Impact of English Towns 1700-1800* states that it was noted in 1750 that 'several of the Market Towns ... being very small, can be reckoned little more than country villages'.

For the following four centuries Solihull continued as a rural backwater, a community somewhere between a town and a village. The effect of various plagues and epidemics, and the resulting economic crises, would have been felt in Solihull as in the rest of Warwickshire, and would have contributed to its decline. It has been estimated that the 14th-century Black Death halved the population of the country as a whole, and the manorial system, which had survived for nearly 300 years after the Norman Conquest, imposing its rules of servile and commuted labour on the population, began to disintegrate as a result of the demographic crisis and the associated rise in wages. The population nationally became restless, with villeins often moving away from villages to towns, but it was inevitable after the enormous number of deaths that there would be a shortage of workers. The 17th-century Warwickshire historian William Dugdale implies that the first visitation of the plague was at its deadliest between May and October 1349, with the highest number of deaths being in the middle of the county. Another epidemic in 1361 probably hit hardest in the west and south-west of the county, and further outbreaks followed in 1369 and 1375-6. The filthy conditions of towns and villages probably contributed to the spread of the pestilence. It was noted in nearby Coventry during one outbreak that 'there remained not the tenth person alive to bury the dead'. Epidemics of other contagious diseases followed in the 16th century, including a 'hot burning fever' which raged through the country killing many people. This fever was probably influenza, and deaths occurred in Solihull between 1557-9 when, for example, William Huband, the rector, died on 6 August 1558. In addition to these alarming epidemic disorders there were several poor seasons in the mid-1550s which resulted in catastrophic harvests.

At the time of the dissolution of the monasteries (which began in 1536), endowments of chantry chapels were also diverted to secular purposes. In Solihull there were various endowments, including those of the chapels of SS Katherine and Mary, and the money which formerly maintained these chapels was used to pay the stipend of a schoolmaster. The first record of this change of use is in 1560 and marks the creation of Solihull Free Grammar School (now known as Solihull School). There is a tradition that the school was founded in the reign of Richard II (1377-99), but as John Burman pointed out in *Solihull and its School* there is no evidence to prove this tradition. Following 1560 other bequests were made by local people which added to the fund already in existence and eventually became known as Solihull Charity Estate. The income from this estate was administered by trustees known as the feoffees, who became a kind of local government with the parish bailiff as their leader.

Solihull was an extensive parish, including the present parish of Shirley and part of the present parish of Olton. Inhabitants were obliged to attend Solihull parish church on Sundays, which brought together people from outlying districts. The manor court continued to exert authority until the mid-17th century, and the parish authorities organised upkeep of highways, poor relief, and law and order. The first workhouse, in Warwick Road, was built by the feoffees and opened in 1742. The introduction of turnpike trusts improved national routes, and Solihull became useful as a place for changing horses and providing refreshment for travellers on the road to Birmingham, after the Warwick Road was turnpiked in 1725-6. There were several coaching inns in the town, such as the *Limerick Castle* (later the *Barley Mow*) which was a regular stop for the Oxford and London coaches. In the late 18th century the Warwick to Birmingham canal was constructed, opening in 1800, but its route lay about a mile to the north of the town centre and it probably made little impact on the town after the initial disruption caused by its construction. It was later to prove useful when Solihull gas-works was built in 1869 alongside the canal, which enabled supplies of coal for the production of gas to be carried by water.

This quiet rural existence, which had endured for centuries, was ultimately to be lost forever by the arrival in the 1850s of the Oxford and Birmingham Railway. Initially, the railway had little impact on the town. Solihull station opened in 1852 and made it possible for businessmen to move to the country while working in Birmingham, but the number of commuters was small at first. In the mid-19th century Solihull had few amenities to offer, but gradually more services were introduced, and more houses were built. Typical migrants were Alfred Bird (later to become a baronet), who was the son of the founder of Bird's Custard, and Joseph Gillott, son of the inventor of the steel pen nib. Bird bought Tudor Grange in 1900, and enlarged the already handsome house, which is now part of Solihull College of Technology in Blossomfield Road; Gillott bought the Berry Hall Farm estate in 1870 and built a new mansion as his home, which is now a neglected ruin. There was much development in the late 19th century, with roads such as Homer Road and Herbert Road built by the 1880s, and Ashleigh Road and The Crescent laid out with large houses before 1914. Further waves of house-building followed in the periods after the First and Second World Wars.

The increase in population affected town government. The original parish of Solihull covered a very large geographical area. In 1831 the Revd. Archer Clive, Rector of Solihull, was instrumental in building a Chapel of Ease at Shirley, and this resulted in the creation in 1843 of the parish of Shirley. Before this date the residents of the Shirley area had to travel to St Alphege's to attend services, and their affairs were administered by the Solihull Parish Vestry. In 1894, following legislation creating the modern system of local government in England and Wales, Solihull was created a Rural District Council (R.D.C.), within the county of Warwickshire. The area administered by the new R.D.C. included the parishes of Solihull, Shirley, Baddesley Clinton, Barston, Lapworth, Balsall, Bushwood, Elmdon, Knowle, Nuthurst, Packwood, and Tanworth-in-Arden. The expansion in population caused by the new houses built in the Edwardian period and in the 1920s led to the creation of Solihull Urban District Council (S.U.D.C.) in 1932, when the more rural areas such as Lapworth were removed. S.U.D.C., operating from offices in the newly converted Council House in Poplar Road (formerly the Public Hall), had more powers than before, but many decisions were still taken by Warwick County Council. In 1954, reflecting further expansion, Solihull was granted a Charter by Queen Elizabeth II and became a Municipal Borough, and in 1964 was granted County Borough status. Until the early 1970s Solihull had always been a part of Warwickshire, but in 1974 under legislation reorganising local government, Solihull Metropolitan Borough Council (S.M.B.C.) was created. S.M.B.C. is one of seven district councils in the West Midlands, and covers a much wider geographical area than ever before, including Castle Bromwich, Kingshurst, Fordbridge, Smiths Wood, Chelmsley Wood, Marston Green, Bickenhill, Elmdon, Hampton-in-Arden, Berkswell, Balsall Common, Barston, Knowle, Meriden, Olton, Solihull, Shirley, Hockley Heath and Temple Balsall.

From 1954 onwards the new Borough Council began to construct civic buildings in Solihull to reflect its increased status. The first building was the Civic Hall (now known as the Conference and Banqueting Centre), opened by Queen Elizabeth II in 1962, and soon followed by the new Council House (to replace the original building in Poplar Road) and Civic Suite. A new police station was constructed in Homer Road, and later a new Magistrates' Court. The new central library and theatre complex opened in 1976, and the Council House was extended in 1988.

Solihull town centre showed little change for hundreds of years. It emerged relatively unscathed from World War Two but major changes occurred in the 1960s. As early as 1956 the newly formed Municipal Borough Council had reached the conclusion that the shopping facilities in Solihull would be inadequate to meet the demands of the estimated expansion in population and consequent increase in road traffic. Therefore Mr. C. R. Hutchinson, the Borough Surveyor, drew up plans for a new road layout replacing the narrow medieval Mill Lane and Drury Lane with a modern shopping precinct. There was much local opposition to the scheme, which involved the demolition of several medieval buildings in Mill Lane and Touchwood Hall, an 18th-century red-brick house in Drury Lane, together with some buildings in Warwick Road and the High Street. However, in 1962 (two years after a public enquiry) the Ministry of Housing and Local Government finally approved the plans, and demolition began. Building work on the new precinct, which was jointly funded by Solihull Borough Council and Norwich Union, commenced in 1964, and the first shops opened in the summer of 1966. The official opening took place on 20 May 1967, when the central area was named Mell Square in honour of the Borough's first Town Clerk, Mr. W. Maurice Mell, who had died suddenly in 1966. In 1975 the police station in Poplar Road was demolished, following the construction of a new building in Homer Road, and the Poplar Way extension was built to link Mell Square with Poplar Road. Mell Square was refurbished in 1987-8, when the buildings were cleaned, the old fountains removed and replaced with a café, and the area was pedestrianised for the first time. At the time of writing plans have been submitted to further increase the shopping facilities in the town centre in the mid-1990s by extending Mell Square and by constructing a new development on the site of the Civic Centre car park.

For several hundred years Solihull can be seen as a quiet country village-cum-town, typical of many in the midlands of England. While it is probably true to say that the inhabitants were mostly preoccupied with their own affairs (local events and day-to-day priorities) and the town was not the setting for momentous events of national importance, it was not totally isolated from the rest of the country. National events affected Solihull as much as the rest of Britain, and there would have been much interaction with its hinterland. Political events, too, left their mark. For instance, a rector of Solihull parish, John de Feckenham, who was the incumbent at the time of the Reformation, refused to accept the new liturgy (despite allegedly being offered the vacant position of Archbishop of Canterbury if he would recant) and was incarcerated in Wisbech Castle. In 1604 Thomas Throckmorton, then lord of the manor, was obliged to sell the lordship (for £1,080) to help pay crippling fines imposed on him for recusancy as a result of his adhering to the Roman Catholic faith and refusing to attend services in his parish church. During the troubled times of the Civil War in the 17th century Solihull was visited by both Parliamentarian and Royalist forces. In the national emergency caused by the Napoleonic Wars and the threat of invasion, Solihull sent men to join the militia (an early form of Home Guard), and Solihull residents participated in both World Wars of the 20th century, fighting abroad and safeguarding the Home Front. The War Memorial in the Square, outside the parish church, lists the names of those who did not return.

The local inhabitants were also willing to participate in national celebrations. A wooden obelisk (no longer surviving) was erected near the Warwick Road, opposite the entrance to Malvern Hall (the present Brueton Avenue), to commemorate the Battle of Waterloo. There were great celebrations for Queen Victoria's Golden and Diamond Jubilees, in 1887 and 1897 respectively, and also for the Coronations of Edward VII, George V and George VI. In more recent times there were parties to celebrate VE Day and VJ Day at the end of World War Two and to celebrate the Coronation of Queen Elizabeth II in 1953. The Queen visited Solihull in 1977 as part of her Silver Jubilee programme.

The following illustrations attempt to give a pictorial history of the town and its immediate vicinity, but necessarily concentrate on the period from the mid-19th century onwards, as few illustrations exist of Solihull before the invention of photography. It is unfortunately the case that there is never enough space to include all the illustrations one would wish, but it is to be hoped that this selection will at least give an impression of the town's long and interesting history.

Bibliography

Bell, Susan, et al, *Solihull as it Was* (1980)

Burman, John, *Solihull and its School* (1949)

Clive, Mary, *Caroline Clive* (1949)

Faulkener, Alan, *The Warwick Canals* (1985)

Hannett, John, *The Forest of Arden* (1863)

Lines, Charles, 'When Solihull really was a village', *Warwickshire and Worcestershire Life* (March 1987)

Lines, Charles, *When Solihull was a Village*, unpublished transcript of a talk given in Solihull Library Theatre (1989)

Malley, Bernard, *Solihull and the Catholic Faith* (1939)

Martineau, Geoffrey, 'Solihull from 1863 and onwards' *Solihull Parish Magazine* (1933-4)

Pemberton, Robert, *Solihull and its Church* (1905)

Powrie, Jean et al, *Olton Heritage* (1986)

Sargent, C. P., *History of Christ Church, Solihull 1825-1975* (1975)

Shepherd, E. C., *The Tower and Bells of Solihull Church* (1950)

Skipp, Victor, *The Origins of Solihull*, 2nd edition (1984)

Solihull Methodist Church (1980)

Tasker, A., *Conservation of Warwickshire* (1990)

Van Wart, Irving, *Souvenir of Old England, by an Anglo-American* (1880)

Victoria County History of Warwick Vol. 2 (1908)

Victoria County History of Warwick Vol. 4 (1947)

Woodall, Joy, *The Book of Greater Solihull* (1990)

Woodall, Joy, and Varley, Mollie, *Looking Back at Solihull* (1987)

Woodall, Joy, and Varley, Mollie, *Solihull Place Names* (1979)

The Town

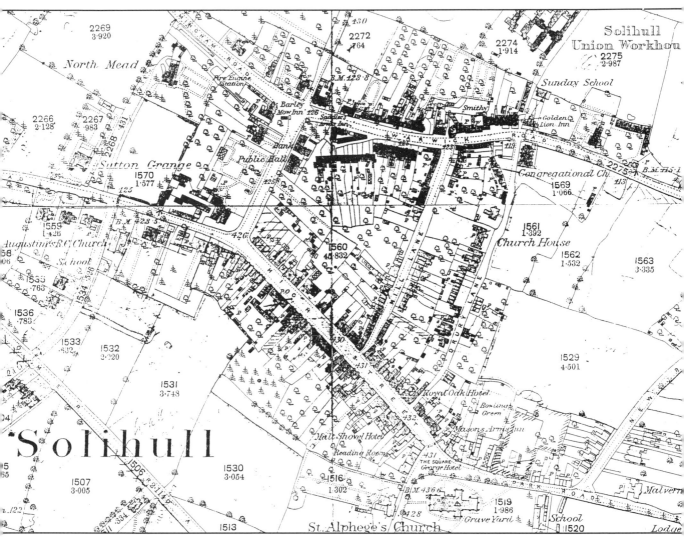

1. Solihull, from first edition Ordnance Survey 25 inch to 1 mile map (1888). Solihull's motto is 'Urbs in Rure' – the town in the country (although the country is now farther away). The long narrow strips of land (some still surviving in the High Street) are evidence of the burgage plots laid out when the town was 'planted' in the 12th century.

2. Solihull High Street *c*.1829, showing a sleepy village: the coach is turning into the narrow Mill Lane by a timber-framed building once the *George and Dragon*; the trees hide the building now known as the Manor House. Pigot's *Directory* 1828-9 notes a Wednesday market '... which has dwindled into insignificance'. In 1821 the population of the parish was 2,817.

3. A view of the High Street *c*.1900 shows remarkably little change in 70 years. As early as 1840, Solihull was described as '... neat and rural in appearance ... an air of comfort and respectability marks all alike and renders Solihull indisputably a delightful looking town'.

4.   The old *George and Dragon*, situated on the corner of the High Street and Mill Lane, before 1887. Davis' baker's shop later occupied the building, which was demolished *c*.1962. Edwin Trinder's chemist's shop is shown on the right. Trinder was a pioneer photographer in the village, together with his son Hugh, and their work is featured in this book.

5.   An early photograph of the High Street, *c*.1870, possibly by Edwin Trinder as it was taken from outside his shop. Houses of different periods, often with narrow frontages, illustrate the original burgage plots. Variations in width could be caused by amalgamations of two or more plots, and the variety of building styles emerged as owners rebuilt at different dates.

6. Early pavements in the High Street were rough cobblestones laid around 1862, and women wore pattens to lift them out of the frequent mud. Later, paving of 'Rowley Rag' was laid in the centre leaving cobblestones at the edge (as in this postcard dated 1915). Loose cobblestones were occasionally used for ammunition by village hooligans, to the detriment of local windows!

7. The top end of the High Street *c.*1913, showing Elcox's fancy goods store (later occupied by Miss Deebanks), and the *Mason's Arms* (left).

8. This unusual view of the High Street was taken by Hugh Trinder from the tower of St Alphege's Church in 1910, and is looking towards Poplar Road. Drury Lane and Mill Lane can be seen on the right and Silhill House is at the top of the picture.

9. A view of the High Street with Ramsgate Cottages and the Post Office on the right. Past the Post Office an archway led to Great Western Mews, where William Ledbrook's services included stabling, smithing, carriage hire (for weddings and funerals), and furniture removals.

10. The Post Office was housed in this building in the High Street from 1828 to 1911 and was in the charge of the Pearman family from 1857. The building on the right was Ramsgate Cottages, which continued at a right angle to the street, with more cottages backing on at the rear.

11. The Manor House, High Street. Formerly known as Lime Tree House (from nine lime trees planted *c*.1720) and never the home of the lord of the manor, it was built by the Greswolds in the late 15th century, and was last occupied by Dr. Ferdinand Page. The Manor House Trust raised £12,000 to save the house in 1945.

12. The Gables, typical of large houses built in the village in the late 19th century, was the home of Dr. Adolphus Bernays in the High Street. It replaced a much earlier house called The Laurels, and was demolished before World War Two. A branch of Woolworth's was built in its place, and Adams Clothing Store occupies the site in 1991.

13. An elegant example of an early 19th-century house in the High Street, probably photographed in the 1870s. Irving van Wart described local society *c*.1814 as consisting of squire and rector, lawyer and curate and ' ...a few ancient spinsters and retired officers who lived in economical gentility and formed the aristocracy of the neighbourhood, composed principally of small farmers'.

14. Typical houses in the High Street between Mill Lane and Drury Lane (now replaced by shops), again showing a variety of architectural styles. The population of the parish in 1841 was 3,333 and in 1871 had only risen to 3,739. The railway station opened in 1852 but growth was gradual until the early 1900s when large scale developments led to rapid increases in population.

15. High Street, 1897, decorated for Queen Victoria's Diamond Jubilee. White's *Directory* of 1874 describes the town as consisting principally of one long street, and continues: 'The houses in general are modern and well-built, and many of them large and handsome. The inhabitants in general are well supplied with water and gas. The air is salubrious, and the surrounding scenery of a pleasing character'.

16. A postcard of 1912 shows the High Street when the cottages at the corner of Poplar Road had been demolished and replaced with these shops. The correspondent was employed in one of the shops, and was not impressed with his new home. He wrote '... the place is very quiet, not a place of amusement in the village'.

17. Moving away from the High Street, a drawing *c.*1820 shows the Square (actually triangular in shape!). Situated at the top of the 'muddy hill' which gave Solihull its name, it was the site of the ancient market. The *George Hotel* is shown (second left) and the village stocks, described by Irving van Wart in his reminiscences, are on the right.

18.   The parish church dates from the 12th century. The Town Hall (right) was built in 1779, replacing a medieval building. Its uses included magistrates' court, assembly hall and jail. Irving van Wart, a pupil at Powell's school in the early 19th century, describes attending dancing classes there with pupils from an adjacent girls' school. The Town Hall was demolished in 1880.

19.   The old houses, usually known as the End Houses, in the Square (shown before 1921). The plaster was removed in 1958, revealing the original brick and timbered construction underneath. Once four dwellings, they are now used as offices. There is a local tradition that one was haunted, but the identity of the ghost has not yet been discovered.

20. St Alphege's school, Park Road, is shown (left) *c.*1905. There has been a school on this site since 1850, when the elementary school for boys was built. In 1862 it was enlarged to accommodate girls and infants and in 1892 the boys were transferred to the new school in Mill Lane to relieve overcrowding.

21. Old cottages in Park Road, *c.*1880s; now the site of the Job Centre. The boy is standing on the corner of New Road, and the distinctive diamond shaped pattern can be seen on the wall of Malvern House.

22. Malvern House, Park Road (shown in the early 20th century), was the home of the Free Grammar School until 1882, when it moved to its present site in Warwick Road. Founded in 1560, it is now known as Solihull School. Geoffrey Martineau (1862-1934) remembered attending when several boys rode to school on ponies, and there was much practical joking when saddling up.

23. New Road, shown *c.*1926 looking towards Warwick Road, was realigned and renamed in 1829. The original route lay farther east in Malvern Park, and was known as Powke Lane in the 18th century (and formerly as Glazewell Lane). It was sometimes called Butte Lane after the village Butts where men were required to practise archery in the 15th and 16th centuries.

24. Solihull Free Grammar School, on its new site in Warwick Road, *c*.1905. It was founded in 1560 (not during the reign of Richard II), although some of the original endowments date from the 14th century, which explains the tradition. Samuel Johnson, who had local connections, was rejected for the post of headmaster in 1735.

25. The interior of Big School *c*.1918 is shown on this postcard. Now a public school, Solihull School has continued to expand on its site in Warwick Road. Famous old boys of the Grammar School include the poets Jago and Shenstone.

26. This view of the Warwick Road, taken after 1882, shows Solihull School on the left and the corner of New Road on the right. Geoffrey Martineau (1862-1934) writing in the 1930s remembered drovers herding cattle through the village along Warwick Road and the High Street.

27. Warwick Road, looking towards the junction with Mill Lane and Whittington's grocer's shop. The tower of the Congregational Church on the corner of Drury Lane, originally known as Dog Lane, can be seen in the distance.

28. Drury Lane, looking towards the Congregational Church on the corner of Warwick Road. Drury Lane and Mill Lane were narrow lanes which linked the High Street and Warwick Road.

29. A view of Mill Lane from Warwick Road, looking towards the High Street (*c*.1911). Mill Lane Boys' School, opened in 1892, can be seen on the left.

30.   Cottages in Drury Lane, *c*.1900. All the buildings in Drury Lane were demolished in the early 1960s to make way for the Mell Square shopping development.

31. Timber-framed cottages in Mill Lane, c.1948. Mill Lane contained several medieval cottages, including this house which may originally have been a hall house. All the buildings in Mill Lane were demolished to make way for the Mell Square development.

32. A view of Warwick Road, looking towards the *Barley Mow* at the junction with Poplar Road and Lode Lane (c.1918). The Post Office transferred to this site in 1911 from its former location in the High Street, and remained here until its removal to Station Road in the 1940s.

33. Solihull Union Workhouse in Union Road was built in 1838. It replaced the earlier workhouse in Warwick Road, and could accommodate 150 inmates by 1874. Twelve parishes formed the Union: Solihull, Baddesley Clinton, Balsall, Barston, Bushwood, Elmdon, Knowle, Lapworth, Nuthurst, Tanworth and Yardley. Solihull Hospital developed from the Workhouse's Infirmary.

34. A view from Poplar Road showing the crossroads with Warwick Road and Lode Lane. The houses at the corner of Lode Lane are the Poplars (left), which had 21 poplar trees in its garden, and the Old Doctor's House (right), which has now been renamed in honour of Paul Quinet who was for many years a surgeon in Solihull.

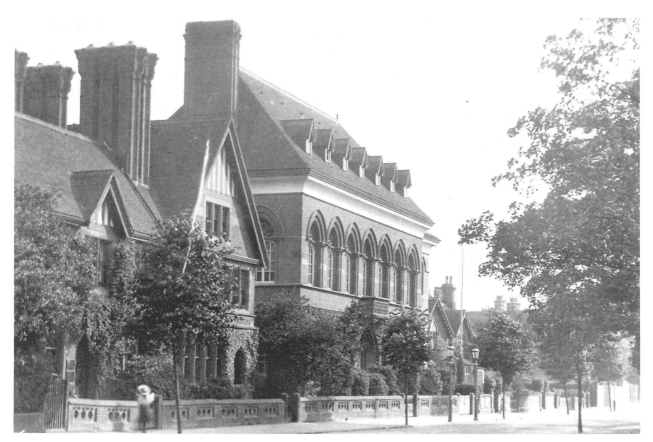

35. Poplar Road, with Lloyds Bank, opened in 1877 as the first bank in the village, on the left, and the old Council House. This was built by private enterprise in 1876 as a Public Hall, and the opening event was a grand ball with a band from London. It was acquired by the local authority in 1919 and opened as the offices for Solihull U.D.C. in 1937.

36. Station Road, from the corner of Herbert Road, c.1912. The large houses on the left, typical of late Victorian and Edwardian expansion in the town, later housed St Martin's School until its removal to Malvern Hall in 1989. Martineau remembered saw-pits near the junction with the Crescent, where a brook washed away the sawdust.

37. The railway came to Solihull in 1852, when the Oxford and Birmingham Railway (later G.W.R.) was opened. The original station was on a site nearer Streetsbrook Road, and was moved to its present site in the 1930s. Shown here in 1864, the line was both broad and standard gauge, until the removal of the broad gauge in 1869.

38. Increased traffic necessitated the enlargement of the station, which included the erection of a footbridge and a signal box, both completed by 1902.

39. Frequent commuter trains to Birmingham enabled businessmen to live in the cleaner environment of Solihull, Olton and Dorridge while working in the city. Many houses were built to meet the demands of the new residents. This photograph shows Edwardian commuters at Solihull Station.

The Country

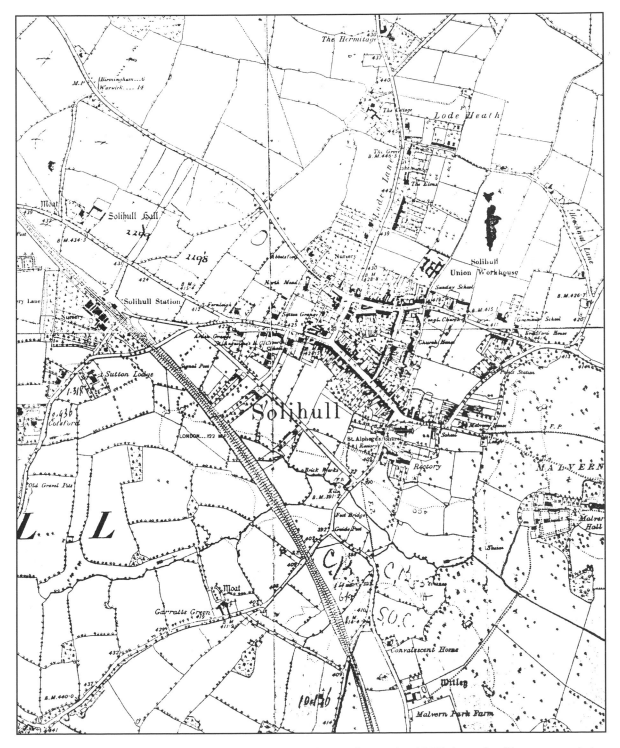

40.   An extract from the first edition Ordnance Survey 6 inch to 1 mile map dated 1888 shows the village surrounded by fields. The surrounding countryside also included heaths and small woods, such as Lode Heath, Browns Coppice, and Shoulder of Mutton Wood. These features illustrate the landscape of the Forest of Arden.

41. The River Blythe flows to the east of Solihull. There was originally a ford and footbridge at Ravenshaw which became a tourist attraction. The ford is now closed to traffic.

42. Sandals Bridge, named after John de Sandale who was Rector of Solihull 1311-16, carried the Warwick Road over the River Blythe. Situated near Malvern Hall, it has been widened in recent years.

43. The ford in Streetsbrook Road, *c.*1907. The ford was situated near the present Woodlea Drive, and the stream ran into Olton Mere. In the 1860s a water carrier named Jimmy Crump fetched water from this stream and others, transporting it in a barrel drawn on a donkey cart to sell in Solihull village for a halfpenny a bucket.

44. Blossomfield Road *c.*1910 was a winding country lane, typical of the roads surrounding the village, but street lights had been installed. Blossomfield Road was known in the 15th century as Wircester Way.

45. Church Hill was the muddy hill upon which Solihull was founded, giving the town its name. In 1915 the road was steeper, with a high footpath. Part of the medieval road from Worcester to Coventry (an important trading centre), it was probably a major influence in the growth of the town, as it brought traders to the town's market.

46. A view across the Rectory meadows in 1897 shows the Rectory and Rectory Farm with the church beyond, and illustrates the proximity of the countryside.

47. Another farm, Whitely Farm in Widney Manor Road, is shown *c*.1900. Sometimes called Malvern Park Farm and built in the late 16th century, the house survives today.

48. Evans' Convalescent Home was originally founded on a small scale in Warwick Road by Miss Caroline Martineau for sick children from West Bromwich. After 1872 Miss Martineau left the district, and the administration of the Home (shown here in 1911 in Widney Manor Road where it was located by 1887) was taken over by Mrs. Evans, wife of Charles Evans, Rector of Solihull 1872-94.

49. Silhill Hall was situated in
Streetsbrook Road, near the junction with
Broad Oaks Road. It probably dated
from the 14th century and was originally
a moated site. Although a Grade I listed
building, it was illegally demolished in
1966. In this photograph the timber
frame was partially covered in plaster
rendering.

50. Silhill Hall originally contained a
great hall, shown here in a conjectural
drawing from the 19th century. The hall
was later divided into smaller rooms.

51. Homer Road, shown here *c*.1900, was named after a local family, resident at a house later known as 'Southend' in Station Road. Conveniently situated for the railway station, it contained several large handsome houses, most of which were demolished to make way for the office developments of the 1980s.

52. Typical of the Edwardian expansion of the village, Ashleigh Road was cut through by 1904, with most houses built by 1910. It has recently been designated a conservation area.

53. Lode Lane, shown here *c.*1900, is described by Geoffrey Martineau in his reminiscences (1933) as a country lane with several deep ditches, which must have been a considerable hazard. Martineau tells of both his aunt and a nursemaid falling into the ditches in separate incidents.

54. Lode Lane crosses the Grand Union Canal near the junction with Dovehouse Lane. The bridge over the canal (which is in a deep cutting at this point) was photographed *c.*1905.

55. The Grand Union Canal (originally the Warwick and Birmingham Canal) opened in 1800. The *Anchor Inn*, in Wharf Lane, shown here on the left, closed in 1937, and has since been demolished. The canal made little impact on Solihull at first as there was no canalside industry, but it was to prove useful in the 1860s when Solihull gas-works opened.

56. The *Anchor Inn* was situated conveniently near to the gas-works, and this photograph shows some of the workers enjoying refreshments in the 1930s.

57. Olton Watermill, Lode Lane, is shown in 1913. Situated on Hatchford brook, the mill was in operation by the end of the 18th century, and still in use in the 1920s. Fed by a large pool to the west of Lode Lane, the mill buildings were on the opposite side of the lane. Demolished by 1969, the site is now part of a housing estate.

58. The present Henwood Mill (shown here c.1947) is an 18th-century building on a very ancient site. A mill on this site formed part of Henwood priory in the late 15th and early 16th centuries. Situated on the river Blythe, this building was occupied by 1860, and milling is said to have continued until the 1930s.

59.   A rear view of Henwood Mill *c*.1900 shows some of the machinery and one of the distinctive dovecotes on the wall. The brick-built building is three stories high, and a breast shot waterwheel was mounted externally. A substantial mill house, also built of brick, adjoins the mill.

60. Moat Farm stood near the junction of Moat Lane and Lode Lane, and is now the site of the Council depot. This photograph was taken before World War II, and the building was demolished by 1963.

61. Old Berry Hall (shown here in an Edwardian postcard) was the moated home of the Waring family from 1505 to 1671. It later became a farm, and is still in existence today.

62. In 1870 Joseph Gillott junior, the Birmingham pen manufacturer, bought the Berry Hall Farm estate, and commissioned the Victorian architect J. A. Chatwin to build a new house for his family in Marsh Lane. The new house was a large mansion with extensive landscaped gardens, but is now a sadly decayed ruin.

63. Ravenshaw Hall, a 15th-century timber-framed, moated homestead situated near the ford on the river Blythe at Ravenshaw, is shown here in 1947. It is now a Grade II listed building.

64. Local rural activity included this timberyard in old Lode Lane, shown here in the early years of this century. The business was owned by Frank Dixon of Borrows Lane, Sheldon, who rented the land from his friend Frank Barber, a local farmer. Mr. Dixon moved his timberyard to Coleshill in 1937. He was killed while crossing the Coventry Road in 1951.

Village Characters

65. James Holliday (1838-1902), last parish beadle of Solihull, at the church door. He also served as parish clerk and sexton; he died on his way to church one Sunday evening, and was buried in his uniform. James and his wife were much in demand at private dances as master-of-ceremonies and cloakroom attendant respectively.

66. Reputed centenarian Granny Leeson is shown here *c.*1881 with her clay pipe. An enthusiastic smoker, visitors were expected to bring her a 'present' of tobacco! Other instances of longevity in the village were recorded in West's *Directory* of 1830, including the Short family: Mr Short, surgeon, then aged 92, his wife, aged 84, and their servant Sally Hames, aged 70.

67. Barber Hopkins' shop was on the corner of Drury Lane and High Street opposite the *Royal Oak* from *c.*1854 to *c.*1900. An unusual feature of a haircut was his habit of asking customers to turn the chair around halfway through to cut the second side. Also a violinist, Charles Hopkins (shown here *c.*1880) provided music for private dances, with his daughter who played the harp.

68. Mr. Thomas Horne, another long-lived pipe smoker and wealthy ironmonger in Birmingham, lived at the Manor House in the late 19th century. A local story relates that he was very particular about his drinking water, paying to have water delivered from a particular spring in Lugtrout Lane (although some doubted the authenticity of the water supply).

69. Hugh Trinder (son of Edwin, the village chemist, and assistant verger at the parish church) outside the chancel door (left) with John Bass (verger), Courtenay Woods (organist) and Mr. Wormald (Rector, 1926-35 seated), c.1930. A keen photographer like his father, Trinder was responsible for many photographs of the village, often walking for miles carrying his camera equipment to record a wedding.

70. Arthur Edward Hobbins, shown outside his shop in Warwick Road, was a watch and clockmaker, and also a photographer. His advertisement follows, and some of his photographs appear in this book. His horological theories seem unorthodox: a local lady was reprimanded for causing a clock to stop by leaving the bedroom window open!

71. Hobbins' advertisement. *c.*1911.

72. Typical of the many weddings held at the parish church, this was the wedding of Miss Winnie Warner from Lugtrout Lane to Mr. Alfred Haldenby of Hull on 24 July 1920.

73.   Residents of Ramsgate Cottages, High Street, *c.*1900. This row was at the rear of the cottages fronting onto the High Street, approached along a path at right angles to the pavement.

74.   Solihull Cricket Club was founded in the mid-1850s, and had a cricket ground at Broomfields.

75. Solihull Football Club, shown here in an Edwardian photograph with the Rector, the Revd. Harvey Brooks, was founded in 1891. The team enjoyed much success between 1912-14. The Club had a football pitch at Broomfields near the Union Workhouse.

Houses and Families

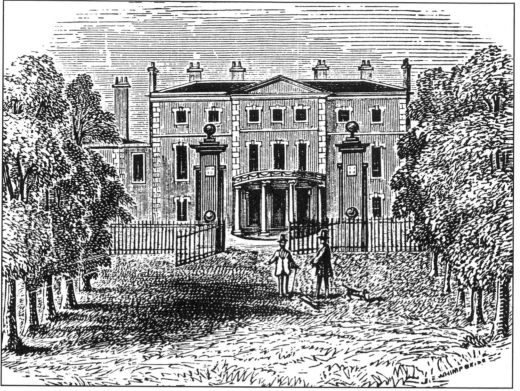

76.   A stately home set in its own parkland (now Malvern Park and Brueton Park), Malvern Hall was built by Humphrey Greswolde in 1702. It was remodelled in the late 18th century by Sir John Soane for Henry Greswolde Lewis, who also commissioned John Constable to paint the Hall and family portraits.

77.   Malvern Hall, shown here from the rear, remained in the Greswolde family until 1896 when David Troman bought it and removed the wings and top storey. The Hall has been used as a girls' school since the 1930s – first Solihull High School for Girls, and later a comprehensive. It has been the home of St Martin's School since 1989.

THE SIXTH FORM COLLEGE, SOLIHULL
THE LEARNING CENTRE

78. Hillfield Hall was built by William and Ursula Hawes in 1576, although a house and farm had been established since about the end of the 13th century. The new house was a status symbol, built of brick at a time when timber-framed buildings were much more common in Warwickshire. The house is now a restaurant.

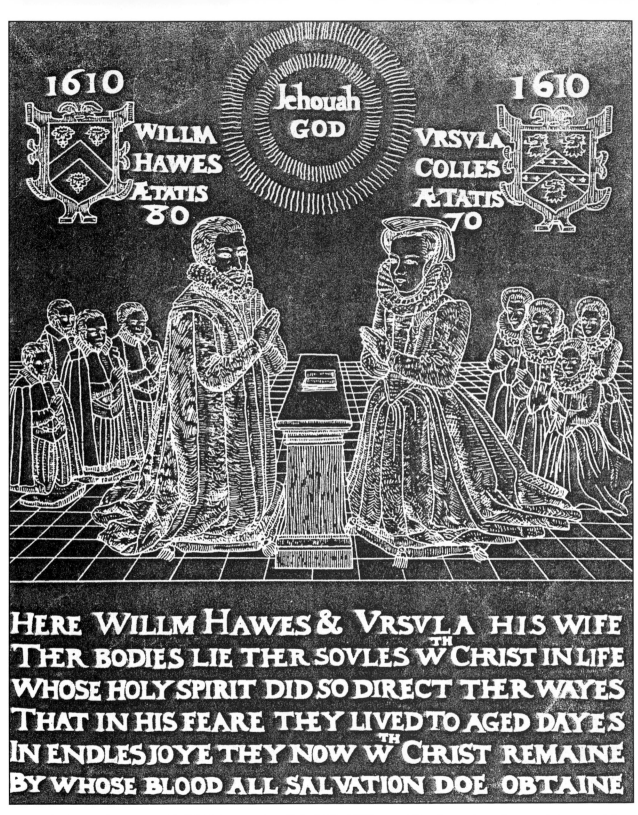

79. The Hawes family owned Hillfield from 1311 until the 1660s. William and Ursula are shown here on their memorial tablet in St Alphege's parish church. This memorial has recently been restored with help from members of the Hawes family in the U.S.A.

80. The original Rectory at St Alphege's church was an Elizabethan timber-framed building. It was demolished during the 1830s by the Revd. Archer Clive, who replaced it with a large brick house at his own expense – having the bricks burnt in a nearby field, thus saving 11 shillings per thousand bricks.

81. Brother of Sir William Curtis (Lord Mayor of London, 1798), Charles Curtis was rector 1787-1829, and rector of St Martin's, Birmingham 1781-1829, preferring to live at Solihull where he could indulge his passion for hunting. A colourful local personality, Curtis was involved in a public argument with Samuel Parr, vicar of Hatton, and enlisted in the local Volunteer Corps.

82.　This large handsome house was built by the Revd. Archer Clive *c*.1834, and served as the rectory until 1933 when it was demolished by the Revd. C. Wormald and replaced with the present building. This view shows the rear of the house, viewed from the garden.

83. The Revd. Archer Clive, rector of Solihull 1829-47, was the son of Edward Bolton Clive, M.P. (a wealthy Herefordshire landowner) and grandson of Lord Archer of Umberslade. This portrait, painted by John Partridge in 1847, was presented to him by his parishioners. During his time at Solihull, Archer used his wealth to effect many improvements in the parish.

84. Caroline Clive (née Wigley), wife of Archer Clive, first came to Solihull in 1829 when her brother Edmund inherited Malvern Hall. A considerable heiress, and crippled from a childhood illness, she lived alone at Olton Hall after Edmund's death until her marriage. Caroline was an authoress, publishing poetry and novels, and she kept a diary recording her life in Solihull.

85. The original Priory (demolished 1889) was a timber-framed building at the top of Church Hill, and was the home of the Hassall family in the 18th century. Powell's School was housed here from 1780 to 1840. A famous pupil was Irving van Wart (nephew of Washington Irving),whose reminiscences, published c.1880, contain descriptions of the school and village.

86. The Mathews family bought the old Priory and demolished it in 1889, having built this large brick house. It is now part of the Council House, and housed Solihull library until 1976 when the new library opened. The name derives from the tradition that nuns from Henwood nunnery were sheltered at the Old Priory after the dissolution.

87. George Mathews, formerly resident at St Bernard's Grange, Olton, was a keen photographer, and left a fascinating record of his farm at Olton and of his family. Mrs Mathews is shown with her children and their friends in this photograph at the Priory.

88. Silhill House, seen here in an early view from the High Street, was situated on the corner of Poplar Road. In the 18th century a coaching inn known as the *Swan* (first mentioned in 1583), it became a private house in the 19th century, and was owned for many years by the Chattock family. The cottages on the right were demolished *c*.1907.

89. Silhill House had a large garden, which extended along Poplar Road almost as far as the *Barley Mow*. A number of outbuildings extended from the house along Station Road, and all were demolished with the house *c*.1926. Memorial tablets record members of the Chattock family at the parish church, where Thomas Chattock and Archer Clive donated the glass in the east window.

90. Tudor Grange was an elegant red-brick mansion built in Blossomfield Road in 1890 by Alfred Lovekin. It was bought in 1901 by Alfred Bird, son of the inventor of Bird's Custard, and was popularly known as 'Custard Hall'. The house is now part of Solihull College of Technology.

91. Sir Alfred Bird (1849-1922), in a portrait by John Seymour Lucas, lived at Tudor Grange until he was killed in a road accident after leaving a political meeting in London in 1922. He was M.P. for Wolverhampton West from 1910 until his death, representing the Conservative Party. One of his hobbies was cycling and he was a founder member of Solihull Cycling Club.

92. Touchwood Hall, shown here *c.*1910, was a red-brick 18th-century house in Drury Lane, built upon an earlier moated site. It was the home of several local families including the Holbeches (whose family memorial tablet may be seen in the parish church), the Madeleys and the Martineaus. The Hall was demolished in 1963 to make way for the Mell Square development.

93. The drawing room at Touchwood Hall in 1900, then the home of the Martineau family. They always left the front door open in the daytime for weary passers-by to walk in and rest. A son of the family was killed abroad in World War One, and afterwards his mother kept a light burning in the window for him.

Public Houses

94.   Named after the former occupation of James Bridge, the first landlord, the *Gardener's Arms* was opened in the High Street in the 1860s and was demolished in 1971. William Lines, landlord from 1892 to 1931, brewed his own ales. The inn was the scene of an unsolved murder in 1880, when an Irishman called John Gately was shot dead in the back yard.

95.   This postcard dated 1915 shows the *Royal Oak Hotel* on the corner of Drury Lane, and the *Malt Shovel* on the left. The *Royal Oak* was built in the 18th century and demolished *c*.1963. The timber-framed *Malt Shovel* is now the *Snooty Fox*.

96. The *George Hotel* in the Square is shown in this postcard with Joe Hillman, landlord at the turn of the century, at the door. Probably dating from the 16th century, the inn was known as the *Nag's Head* from 1693 to 1715 and then became the *Bell*, until changing to its present name in 1738. It was once a coaching inn.

97. The ancient bowling green behind the *George Hotel* is shown here on a postcard of 1906, with its topiary peacock on the right. The green is reputed to have been made in 1693 when Dog Lane Croft was added to the property of the *George*. In his diary, Archer Clive frequently mentions attending Bowling Club dinners.

98. In this photograph the *Golden Lion* in Warwick Road is decorated for the Diamond Jubilee of Queen Victoria in June 1897. Henry Edginton, the whiskered gentleman, sixth from the left, wearing a cap, was the landlord, and he organised an ox roast to celebrate the event. The old inn was replaced by the present building in the 1930s.

99. The *Saddler's Arms* in Warwick Road is shown in a late 19th- century photograph, which was probably taken by Arthur Hobbins.

100. Formerly known as the *Limerick Castle*, and entered down steps, the old *Barley Mow* (shown here in the 1890s) was an important coaching inn. A regular stop for the Warwick, Oxford and London coaches, it was here that the young Irving van Wart arrived on his way to Powell's School *c*.1820, after travelling from his home in Birmingham. The small building in front of the inn was a weigh-house, built in 1833.

101. In 1899 Showell's Brewery partially rebuilt the *Barley Mow*, shown here on a postcard *c*.1920. The turret has since been removed.

Victorian and Edwardian Celebrations

102. This photograph shows an ox roast in Drury Lane at one of the mop fairs in the late 19th century. Until then, a fair was held in the Square, with swing boats and roundabouts. A popular attraction was a pair of dancing bears.

103. In days when there were few holidays, and the luxury of going away for a visit or vacation was the prerogative of the wealthy, seasonal celebrations were very important to local inhabitants. The ancient custom of celebrating May Day continued into the late 19th century. This photograph shows local girls in 1878, possibly in Malvern Park.

104. Local customs included the traditional Maypole, shown here possibly in Malvern Park (not a public park at the time), and the 'May Day Revels' in which chimney sweeps and their assistants dressed up in costume and danced around the village collecting money. One costume was the 'Jack-in-the-Green', a large wicker framework covered with boughs, which concealed a boy.

105. This postcard shows the Christmas fare at the *Mason's Arms* in Solihull High Street in 1908, when Joseph Walker (who catered for this buffet) was the landlord. The *Mason's Arms* appears in trade directories from 1828 onwards, and was owned by licensees until 1903 when it was bought by Holders Brewery of Birmingham.

106. The Public Hall in Poplar Road was built with money raised by public subscription in 1876, and replaced the old Town Hall in the Square. It was the scene of many social and charitable events, such as this bazaar held in 1900.

107. A team was formed at the parish church in 1892 to ring handbells, which required great skill and was very popular *c*.1890-1900. The team played at social functions, visited large houses at Christmas, and gave concerts accompanied by the church organist. The church's fine peal of 10 bells would also be rung in celebration of great events.

108. Local inhabitants joined enthusiastically in national celebrations in addition to local events. This floral arch was erected in the High Street as part of the celebrations for Queen Victoria's Golden Jubilee in 1887.

109. A more elaborate floral arch, also in the High Street, was erected in honour of Queen Victoria's Diamond Jubilee in 1897, and again to celebrate the Coronation of King Edward VII and Queen Alexandra in 1902 (shown in this photograph).

110. Viewed from the roof of Silhill House, this procession was in celebration of the Coronation of King George V
and Queen Mary in 1911. The procession was led by the local clergy and included the town band and a horse-drawn
fire engine. The programme of events also included athletics, a children's tea and a firework display at dusk.

2. SOLIHULL CORONATION PROCESSION.

111.   A closer view shows the procession in the Square, where a crowd had gathered to watch its progress. The procession also included many members of local societies (often carrying their banners) and local members of the armed forces.

Churches

112.   Solihull parish church from the north-east *c*.1860. Dedicated to St Alphege, a Saxon archbishop of Canterbury martyred by the Danes in 1012, the church is a local landmark situated at the top of the 'muddy hill'. Founded by the 12th century, it was enlarged by the de Limesi and Oddingsell families, lords of the manor and founders of Solihull.

113. St Alphege's church is a large and beautiful building, which has benefited from many donations and bequests. It has been restored several times, notably after the collapse of the spire in 1757, which caused much damage. This postcard shows the interior in 1908.

114. This group photograph taken outside the chancel door shows the rector 1893 to 1926, the Revd. T. B. Harvey Brookes (seated, left) and the Revd. C. O. R. Wormald (standing, left), appointed curate in 1903 and later to return as rector. One of the other curates may be the Revd. Robert Pemberton, also appointed in 1903, who was the author of *Solihull and its Church*, published in 1905.

115. The first Methodist church in Solihull (shown here in 1982) opened for public worship on Wednesday 15 February 1905. The church, built at a total cost of £1,748 7s. 3d., seated 150 people. From 1883 to 1905 Methodist services were held in the Public Hall, and before that meetings were held in Blossomfield Farmhouse.

116. A new Methodist church was built on the corner of Station Approach in the 1930s at a cost of £10,000. A marshy site, this has proved an unfortunate choice. The old chapel was sold to Solihull Council c.1960 (the proceeds financing the Church Hall), and was used by the Council for Voluntary Service. It has recently become Solihull Adult Education Centre.

117. The first post-Reformation Roman Catholic chapel in Solihull was built on land given in 1760 by Hugford Hassall (of the Priory), 10 years after the first 'mission'. St Augustine's church, shown here c.1897, replaced the earlier chapel in 1839. Designed by A. W. N. Pugin, it has been much altered, and was the location of the first motorised wedding in Britain in 1897.

118. Independents in Solihull originally held meetings in two cottages in Drury Lane. William Hood was appointed as the first pastor in 1825, and this chapel was opened in Union Road in November 1826. It was used until the Congregational church was built in 1883, after which it became a schoolroom. It was demolished in 1965-6.

119. By 1883 the Bethesda chapel was too small for the growing number of inhabitants in the area. The foundation stone of the new Congregational church (shown here in 1926) was laid in May 1883, and it opened in March 1884. The total cost of the building was £2,671.

120. The Congregational church on the corner of Drury Lane was built in the English Gothic style. It was demolished in 1965-6, following the erection of the building now known as Christ Church United Reformed church (renamed following the union of the Congregational and Presbyterian churches). The interior is shown in 1926.

Public Services

121. The horse-drawn fire engine is seen during Queen Victoria's Diamond Jubilee celebrations in 1897. Solihull and District Volunteer Fire Brigade was formed in 1880, before which date assistance was given by the Birmingham Brigade. Until 1880 the fire engine was housed at the old Town Hall, and was then moved to the Fire Station at the *Barley Mow*.

122. Charles Bragg, shown here early this century, was Captain of the Fire Brigade in the 1890s. Geoffrey Martineau, writing in the 1930s, remembered several fires, including those at Hillfield Hall (1869), Silhill Hall (1866 and 1887), and the Hermitage (1905). There was even a case of arson when suffragettes burnt a house in Warwick Road in 1912.

123. Four generations of fire engines are shown in this photograph, taken in 1931. The fire engine was kept in Streetsbrook Road from 1916, and the present Fire Station was opened in 1934.

124. Construction of the Workhouse Infirmary, probably by workers from Braggs Builders. An old-established Solihull firm, Braggs had premises in Drury Lane in the 19th century, and later there was a builders' yard in Church Hill Road. The Infirmary became Solihull Hospital.

125. Solihull gas-works was constructed alongside the Grand Union Canal in 1869, enabling street lighting to be provided in the town. Many elegant lamps can be seen in photographs of the town. Gas lights were also installed inside buildings, such as the Grammar School and most public houses. W. H. Auden refers to Solihull gas-works in his poem *Prologue at 60*.

126. Solihull Rural District Council was created under the Local Government Act 1894, and replaced the former Rural Sanitary Authority. The R.D.C. was responsible for many services including sanitation, public works, education and health. The R.D.C. dustcart is shown here in Olton, decorated for May Day 1904.

127. The Rural District Council had a responsibility to maintain roads – many country roads were difficult to use in bad weather, because of deep ruts. Geoffrey Martineau described seeing a horse and trap where the wheels were up to the hubs in mud. This steam roller was photographed in Lyndon Road, Olton, in 1904.

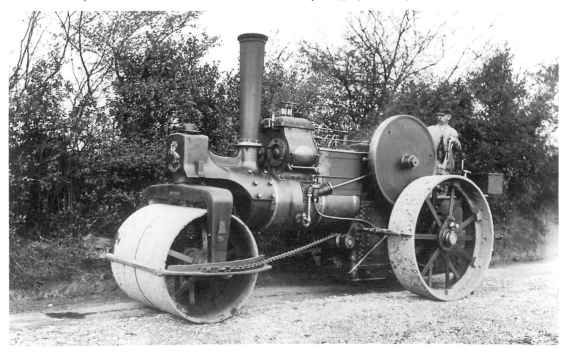

128. These roadmenders were working in Knowle in 1929, when A. E. Currall had been the R.D.C.'s Surveyor for over 30 years. Mr. Currall was often seen driving round the district in his pony and trap.

129. The first police station was built in New Road in 1851, and at the time was the only building in the road.
It was enlarged in 1857, but was still unsatisfactory as the policeman and his family had to share the
building with the prisoners' cells. The building is shown here in 1947, when it was in use as shops.

130. Following sanitary problems at the old lock-up, the authorities built a new police station in Poplar Road, which was in use from 1892 to 1970, when the present building in Homer Road was opened, and this building demolished. Part of the Poplar Way extension to Mell Square now stands on the site.

131. Magistrates sat in various buildings in the town including the old Town Hall in the Square and the *George Hotel*. This building was the first purpose-built courthouse in Solihull, situated on the Warwick Road. It was in use from 1935 to 1981, when the present Magistrates' Court building was opened in Homer Road.

World War I

132. Many young men from Solihull went to fight in the Great War. Among them was Jack Webb, seated third from the left, and shown here with his wife and family outside Deebanks Buildings, Warwick Road. His mother (seated third from the right) was a local midwife.

133. The absence of many young men gave women more opportunities to work. This unknown lady was delivering bread for Cooper's Bakery outside Mr Hobbins' shop (right) in Warwick Road.

134. The Hermitage, in Lode Lane, was built as a private house in 1869, and was the home of Canon Evans before he became Rector of Solihull. Rebuilt after a serious fire in 1905 it became a Red Cross hospital where wounded soldiers were sent to convalesce. The Hermitage is now the centre of a development for the elderly.

135. Miss Townshend (shown here *c.*1916, centre front row) was the Commandant at the Red Cross Hospital at the Hermitage. Dr. Whitehouse from Solihull was the doctor in charge, and in 4½ years, 2,122 patients were treated.

136. Many organisations, both civilian and military, awarded certificates at the end of the War. Miss Hamilton Smith lived in the Solihull area all her life, and was a pupil of Edith Holden at Solihull School for Girls at the time when Edith was compiling her famous nature notes, later published as *The Country Diary of an Edwardian Lady*.

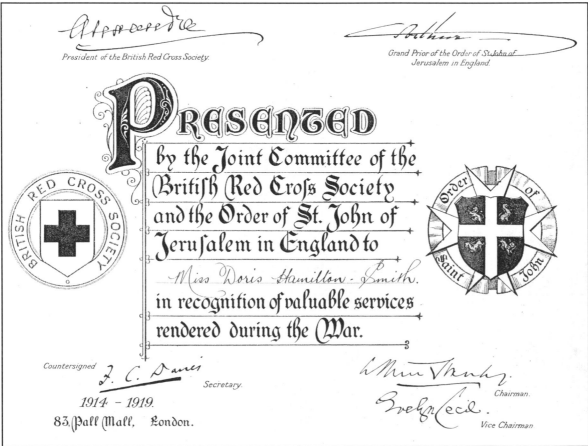

President of the British Red Cross Society.

Grand Prior of the Order of St.John of Jerusalem in England.

Presented

by the Joint Committee of the British Red Cross Society and the Order of St. John of Jerusalem in England to

Miss Doris Hamilton-Smith

in recognition of valuable services rendered during the War.

Countersigned

Secretary.

1914 – 1919.

83, Pall Mall, London.

Chairman.

Vice Chairman

137. Solihull War Memorial was designed by W. H. Bidlake, and erected in the Square in 1921. It is shown here on a postcard dated 1922, with the *George Hotel* and Park Road.

138. The War Memorial was dedicated at a solemn service on 19 June 1921. It was unveiled by the Earl of Craven and dedicated by the Bishop of Birmingham. A firing party fired three volleys, the Last Post was sounded, and Dr. Bernays read the list of the fallen.

1920s and 1930s

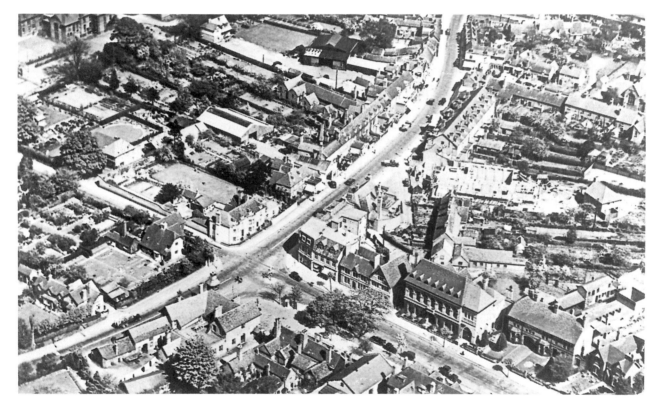

139.   This postcard dated 1934 shows the Council House, soon to open as the offices of Solihull Urban District Council (centre right). The outbuildings behind the *Barley Mow* have now been replaced by a car park, The Poplars opposite has made way for Brueton Gardens, and Blenheim Court now stands in the former gardens of the Doctor's House.

140. In 1930 the parish church bells were recast and rehung in modern fittings. Geoffrey Martineau of Touchwood Hall (left) was Ringing Master from 1891, when he founded the Solihull Guild of Amateur Ringers, until his death in 1934. Roland Bragg (right) succeeded Martineau as Ringing Master.

141. A view of the High Street in 1926 shows little change from the Edwardian views. The large lime trees remain outside the Manor House and Silhill House is still visible in the distance.

142. A view of the High Street in 1935 shows the Parade, built on the corner of Poplar Road and Station Road replacing Silhill House, which was demolished around 1926. Ramsgate Cottages, painted in imitation timber framing, are still visible on the left.

143. Another view of the Parade, showing the shops in Poplar Road.

144. George Road in the 1930s was a quiet road, but more inhabitants were becoming proud owners of motor cars.

145. A view of Warwick Road in the 1930s shows little change to the *Barley Mow*, but the *Saddler's Arms* (left) has been remodelled, and Roger's Garage has been opened (right) to cater for the needs of the growing number of motorists.

146. The Rima Teashop in Mill Lane was a popular meeting-place. The building was timber-framed and was demolished in the early 1960s when the Mell Square development was built.

147.   The Girls' Friendly Society had an active branch in Solihull, and this photograph shows a group outing in the 1920s.

148.   Solihull Carnival procession in the High Street in 1932. Ramsgate Cottages are on the right. The Carnival raised money for a much-needed hospital, but World War Two intervened before it was built.

149. A typical private celebration of the 1920s was the wedding of Mr. and Mrs. Coton at St Alphege's church in 1929. Like the Braggs, the Cotons were a large and well-known local family.

150. There was much expansion in the years after the First World War. The presence of the railway station and the commuter service to Birmingham was an attraction that persuaded more families to move to Solihull. Whitefields Road is shown here c.1919.

151. Streetsbrook Road was another popular residential area conveniently situated for Solihull Station. This postcard shows part of the road c.1920.

World War II

152. Many men and women from Solihull were engaged in active service. This photograph shows Victor Allen from Solihull (seated on right-hand motor cycle) at a training camp near Carlisle, where he was an instructor. Victor and his son George were called up at the same time, and George saw active service in Africa.

153. For those left at home there were several options for war work. This group photograph shows the local Air Raid Precautions Wardens. Most residents erected air raid shelters, but Solihull was considered to be a relatively safe area, and received evacuees from other areas.

154. There were opportunities for women as well as men. The Girls' Training Corps are shown here at Malvern Hall in 1944 where they practised drill and took lessons in cookery and First Aid in readiness for the forces. They also had rifle practice at Solihull Boys' School, and sometimes undertook special duties such as selling programmes at a Glenn Miller charity concert.

155.   Members of the Home Guard are shown here in a parade at the Council House in Poplar Road, possibly on VE day, 8 May 1945.

156.   This photograph shows the Fire Station in Streetsbrook Road *c*.1940, before modern extensions had been built. The building had been opened in 1934 and served a wide area during World War Two. An observer commented on a crew from Solihull fighting to try to save Coventry Cathedral on the night of its destruction.

157.   Women formed a large part of the work force at this time. Local war work included the Brook Tool Factory in Warwick Road. Some of the workers are shown here in a group photograph. There was also the Rover 'Shadow Factory' in Lode Lane (manufacturing aircraft components) which became the famous car factory after the war.

158.   This photograph shows workers at Brook Tool celebrating a wartime Christmas.

159.   Great celebrations followed the announcement of the end of the War in Europe. This party was held in Mill Lane at the British Restaurant (formerly Mill Lane Boys' school) on VE Day.

160. A smaller party was held in Damson Lane for local residents to celebrate VE Day.

Post-War Development

161. The Coronation of H. M. Queen Elizabeth II was the first major national event in the post-war era to offer the opportunity for great celebrations. This photograph shows the official parade passing the Council House in Poplar Road.

162. The Council House, Poplar Road, decorated in honour of Charter Day, 1954. Still in existence, though reduced in size, the building now houses the Area Health Authority.

163. H. R. H. Princess Margaret presented the Charter of Incorporation on behalf of H. M. the Queen on 11 March 1954 to the Mayor designate, Councillor R. D. Cooper. The Charter created Solihull Municipal Borough and gave Solihull a Mayor for the first time in over 300 years. Seated to the right of Councillor Cooper is W. Maurice Mell, the Borough's first Town Clerk, after whom Mell Square is named.

164. H. M. Queen Elizabeth II
unveiling a plaque to
commemorate the official opening
of the Civic Hall (now the Solihull
Conference and Banqueting
Centre), May 1962. The Civic Hall
was the first civic building to be
completed, and was followed by the
Council House, Civic Suite, the
police station, magistrates court,
the library/theatre complex and
(most recently) by the Council
House extension.

165. The Conference and Banqueting Centre, Council House and Civic Suite in 1991. The Council House and Civic Suite
were in use by 1968, and replaced the original Council House (once the Public Hall) in Poplar Road.

166.   In 1962 Solihull was created a County Borough, which gave more power to the local Council. The Mayor and Councillors are shown in this group photograph *c*.1963 outside the Civic Hall, together with the Town Clerk, W. Maurice Mell.

167. By 1956 the town planners considered that the shopping centre would be inadequate in view of the expected expansion in population and increase of traffic (shown here in the High Street in the 1950s). The Borough Surveyor drew up preliminary plans for a new shopping development.

168.   The plans for the new development involved demolishing all the buildings in Mill Lane and Drury Lane, and some of Warwick Road and High Street. Despite much local opposition, permission was granted by the Ministry of Housing and Local Government in 1962, and site clearance began in 1963. This photograph shows the demolition of medieval buildings in Mill Lane.

169.   Building commenced in 1964, and the first shops opened in the summer of 1966. The official opening of the completed development (shown here in 1991) took place on 20 May 1967, when it was named in honour of the late Town Clerk. Poplar Way opened in 1978 and Mell Square was refurbished and pedestrianised in 1987-8.

170. The extension to the Council House, named Orchard House, was built in 1989, and is the most recent civic building to be completed in the town centre.

171. *Brookes Hotel* (left) and the National Homeloans headquarters in Homer Road (1991) are typical of present-day development taking place in and around the town centre.

172. The Square, the War Memorial and the newly restored *George Hotel* (right), photographed on a Sunday morning in April 1991. Although many older buildings have now disappeared and been replaced with larger-scale modern office developments, the Square, once the heart of the medieval town, still reflects the former character of Solihull.